Pebble® Plus

## Understanding Differences

# Some Kids Use
# Wheelchairs

### Revised Edition

4D

Download the
Capstone 4D app
for additional content.

4D  See page 2
for directions.

by Lola M. Schaefer

CAPSTONE PRESS
a capstone imprint

# Download the Capstone 4D app!

- Ask an adult to search in the Apple App Store or Google Play for "Capstone 4D".
- Click Install (Android) or Get, then Install (Apple).
- Open the app.
- Scan any of the following spreads with this icon:

When you scan a spread, you'll find fun extra stuff to go with this book!
You can also find these things on the web at www.capstone4D.com
using the password: wheelchairs.09984

Pebble Plus is published by Capstone Press,
1710 Roe Crest Drive, North Mankato, Minnesota 56003
www.mycapstone.com

**Library of Congress Cataloging-in-Publication Data is
available on the Library of Congress website.**
ISBN 978-1-5435-0998-4 (library binding)
ISBN 978-1-5435-1002-7 (paperback)
ISBN 978-1-5435-1006-5 (ebook pdf)

**Editorial Credits**
Sarah Bennett, designer; Tracy Cummins, media researcher;
Tori Abraham, production specialist

**Photo Credits**
Capstone Studio: Karon Dubke, 7, 13, 15, 17, 19; Getty Images:
KidStock, 9; Newscom: Leah Warkentin/Design Pics, 21;
Shutterstock: DoozyDo, Design Element, Jaren Jai Wicklund,
Cover, 5, 11

## Note to Parents and Teachers

The Understanding Differences set supports national social
studies standards related to individual development and
identity. This book describes and illustrates children who use
wheelchairs. The images support early readers in understanding
the text. The repetition of words and phrases helps early readers
learn new words. This book also introduces early readers to
subject-specific vocabulary words, which are defined in the
Glossary section. Early readers may need assistance to read
some words and to use the Table of Contents, Glossary, Read
More, Internet Sites, Critical Thinking Questions, and Index
sections of the book.

Printed in the United States of America.
010775S18

# Table of Contents

# Why Kids
# Use Wheelchairs

Some kids use wheelchairs.

Kids who cannot walk use

wheelchairs to go places.

Some kids cannot walk because

they were born with weak

bones or muscles.

Other kids use wheelchairs

after they get hurt.

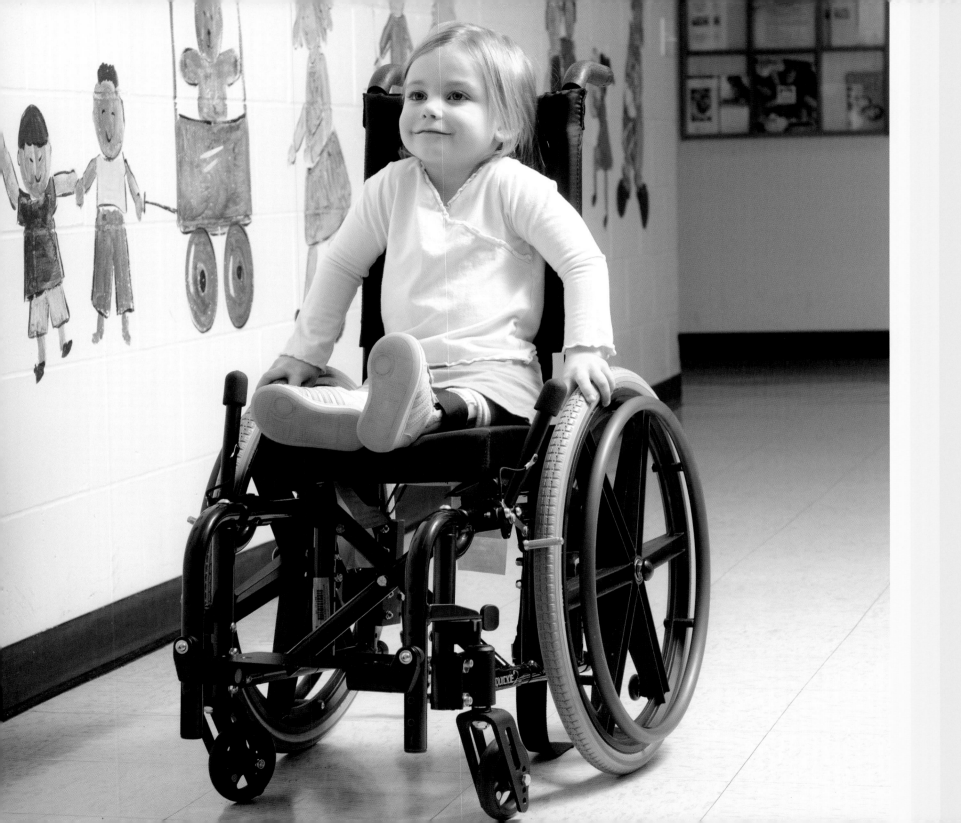

# Being Active

Physical therapists help kids who use wheelchairs stretch their muscles.

Some kids who use wheelchairs go swimming. The exercise is good for their muscles.

11

# Everyday Life

Kids who use wheelchairs go
many places.
They use ramps to get
into vans.

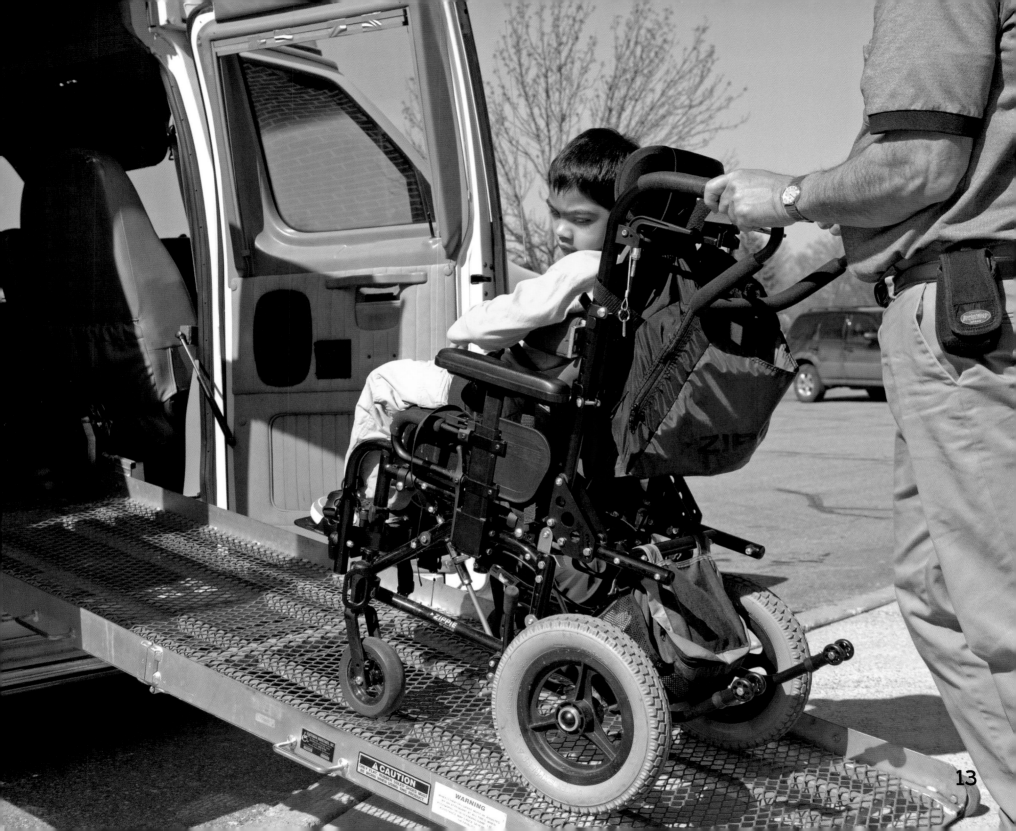

They use ramps to enter
and exit buildings.

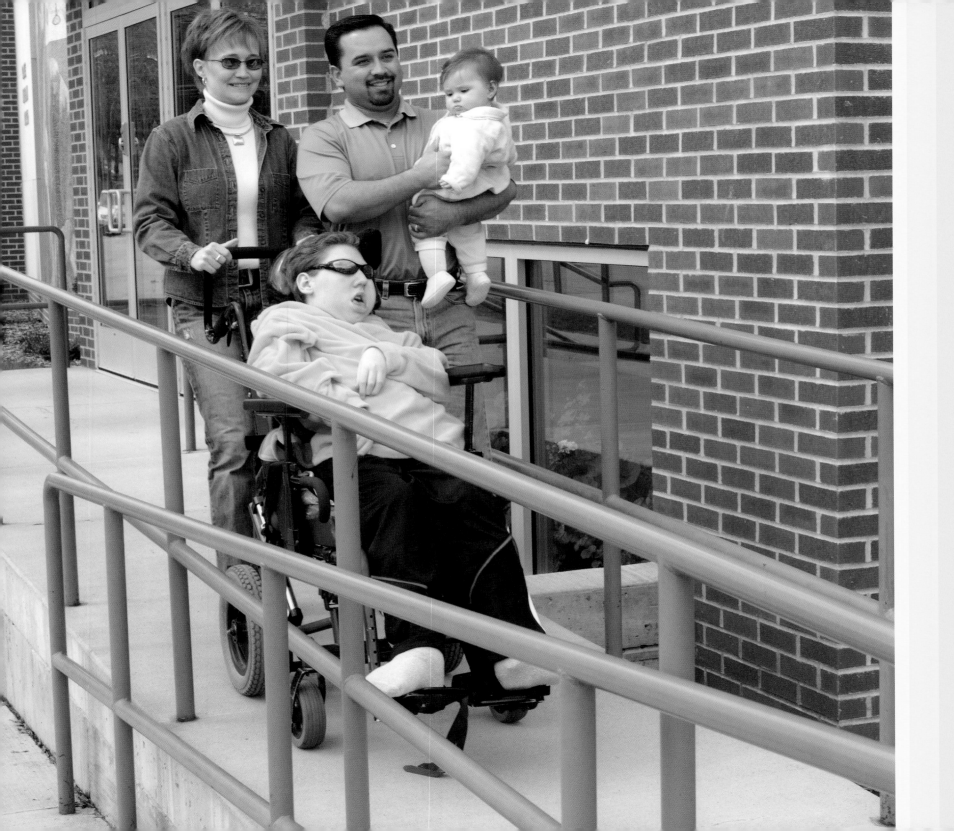

Kids who use wheelchairs

go to the library.

They read books and

use computers.

Some kids who use wheelchairs play sports.

Some kids who use wheelchairs

go skateboarding.

They have fun!

# Glossary

**physical therapist**—a person trained to give treatment to people who are hurt or have physical disabilities; massage and exercise are two kinds of treatment

**ramp**—a flat area that slants to connect two levels; ramps allow people in wheelchairs to get into buildings and vans

**wheelchair**—a type of chair on wheels for people who are ill, hurt, or have physical disabilities; wheelchairs can be pushed by hand or by motor

# Read More

**Burcaw, Shane.** *Not So Different.* New York: Roaring Brook Press, 2017.

**English, James Edward.** *Galia's Dad Is in a Wheelchair.* Fort Worth, Texas: TCU Press, 2017.

**Poole, Hilary W.** *Disability and Families.* Families Today. Broomall, Penn.: Mason Crest, 2017.

# Internet Sites

Use FactHound to find Internet sites related to this book.

Visit *www.facthound.com*

Just type **9781543509984** and go.

Super-cool stuff! Check out projects, games and lots more at www.capstonekids.com

# Critical Thinking Questions

1. What does a physical therapist do?

2. What are some reasons a person may need to use a wheelchair?

3. Why are ramps important to people who use wheelchairs?

# Index